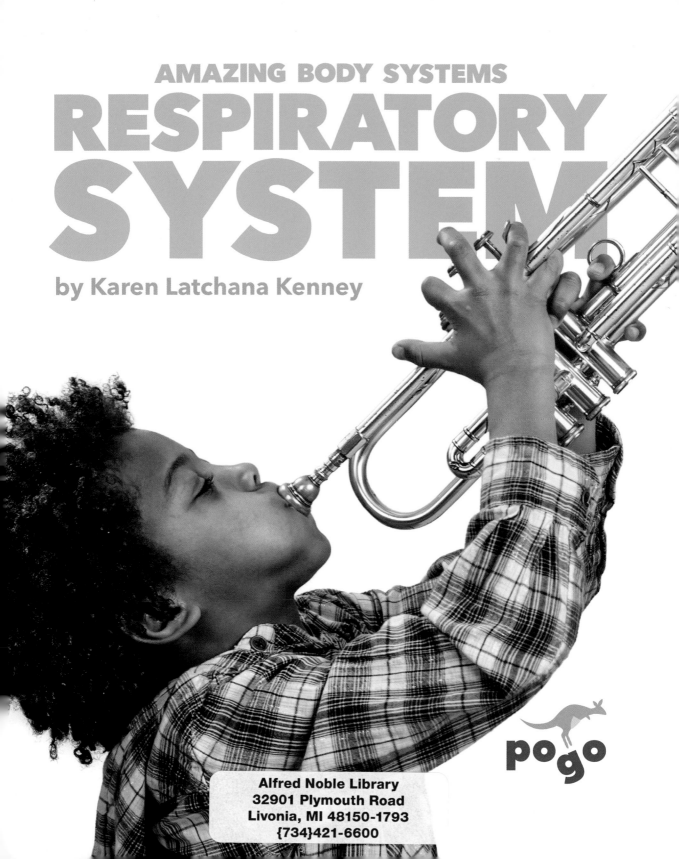

AMAZING BODY SYSTEMS

RESPIRATORY SYSTEM

by Karen Latchana Kenney

pogo

Ideas for Parents and Teachers

Pogo Books let children practice reading informational text while introducing them to nonfiction features such as headings, labels, sidebars, maps, and diagrams, as well as a table of contents, glossary, and index.

Carefully leveled text with a strong photo match offers early fluent readers the support they need to succeed.

Before Reading

- "Walk" through the book and point out the various nonfiction features. Ask the student what purpose each feature serves.
- Look at the glossary together. Read and discuss the words.

Read the Book

- Have the child read the book independently.
- Invite him or her to list questions that arise from reading.

After Reading

- Discuss the child's questions. Talk about how he or she might find answers to those questions.
- Prompt the child to think more. Ask: What other body systems do you know about? What do they do? How might they interact with the respiratory system?

Pogo Books are published by Jump!
5357 Penn Avenue South
Minneapolis, MN 55419
www.jumplibrary.com

Library of Congress Cataloging-in-Publication Data

Names: Kenney, Karen Latchana, author.
Title: Respiratory system / by Karen Latchana Kenney.
Description: Minneapolis, MN: Jump!, Inc. [2016]
Series: Amazing body systems
Audience: Ages 7-10. | Includes index.
Identifiers: LCCN 2016030805 (print) | LCCN 2016031650
(ebook) | ISBN 9781620315613 (hardcover: alk. paper)
| ISBN 9781620316016 (pbk.) | ISBN 9781624965098
(ebook)
Subjects: LCSH: Respiration--Juvenile literature.
Lungs--Juvenile literature. | CYAC: Respiratory system.
Classification: LCC QP121 .K36 2016 (print) | LCC QP121
(ebook) | DDC 612.2--dc23
LC record available at https://lccn.loc.gov/2016030805

Series Editor: Jenny Fretland VanVoorst
Series Designer: Anna Peterson
Photo Researcher: Anna Peterson

Photo Credits: All photos by Shutterstock except:
Alamy, 10; Dreamstime, cover; Getty, 4-5, 8-9, 18-19;
SuperStock, 17, 20-21.

Printed in the United States of America at
Corporate Graphics in North Mankato, Minnesota.

TABLE OF CONTENTS

CHAPTER 1
Your Lungs......................................4

CHAPTER 2
Breathe In.................................. 10

CHAPTER 3
Breathe Out................................ 16

ACTIVITIES & TOOLS
Try This!.....................................22
Glossary 23
Index..24
To Learn More..............................24

CHAPTER 1

YOUR LUNGS

You breathe in. You breathe out.
You do this every second of every day.

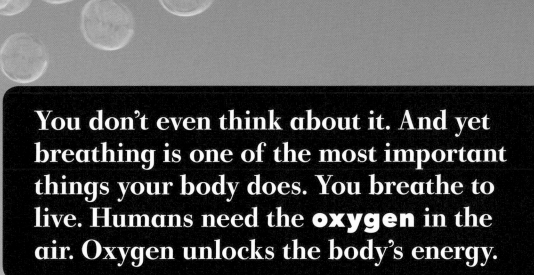

You don't even think about it. And yet breathing is one of the most important things your body does. You breathe to live. Humans need the **oxygen** in the air. Oxygen unlocks the body's energy.

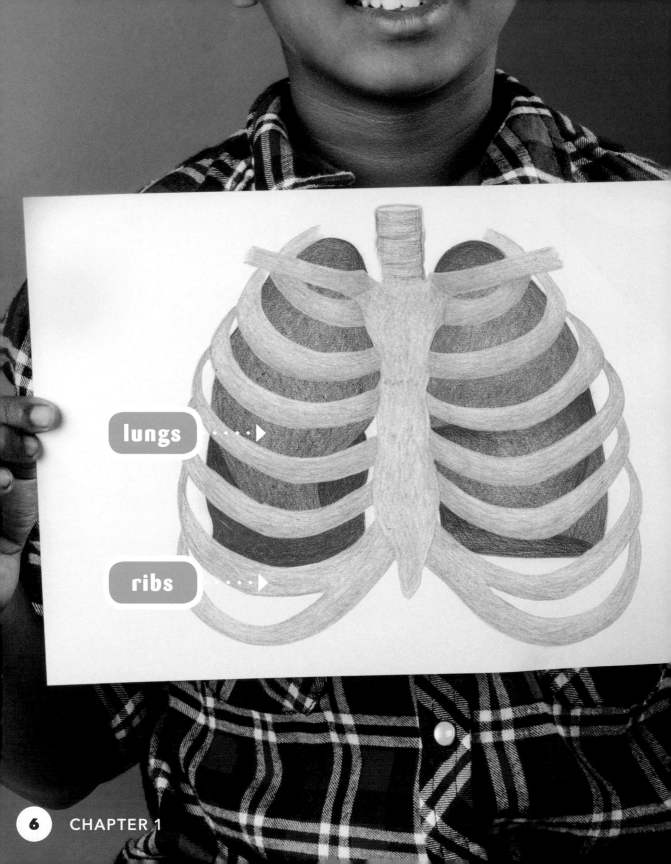

lungs ····▶

ribs ····▶

The **respiratory system** controls breathing. The **lungs** are the central **organs** of this body system. They are two large, spongy organs. They sit in your chest. Strong bones called ribs cover your lungs. They keep the soft organs safe.

TAKE A LOOK!

The respiratory system is in the upper body and head.

Each lung has sections called **lobes**. They grow and shrink with each breath. They're a bit like balloons.

The **diaphragm** lets the lungs fill with air. This muscle tightens and drops down. Now the lungs have more space to grow. This lets you **inhale**.

lobe

lobe

diaphragm

CHAPTER 2
BREATHE IN

Inhaling brings air into the body. Most air enters through your nose.

inhale

Tiny hairs and sticky **mucus** trap dirt and germs. The air gets clean, warm, and moist.

The air moves into a tube known as the windpipe. See how the tube splits? These are the **bronchi**. Each goes into a lung.

Inside the lungs, the tubes get smaller and smaller. These **bronchioles** look like branches on a tree.

DID YOU KNOW?

Most people breathe up to 23,000 times each day!

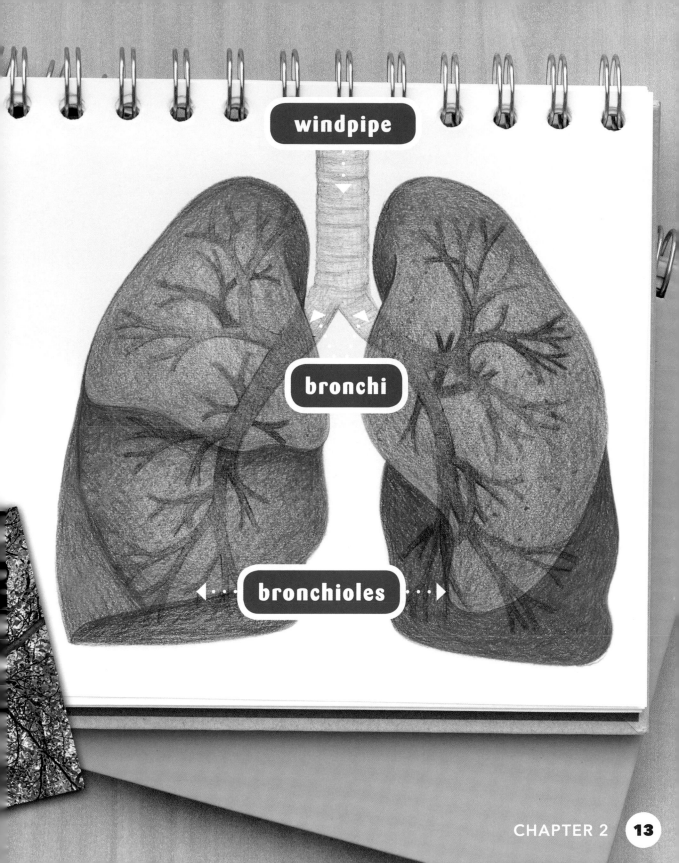

alveoli

capillaries

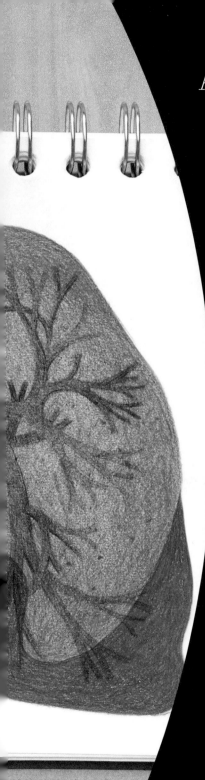

At the end of these tubes are tiny sacs called **alveoli**. They fill with air.

Veins run through the lungs. They become small **capillaries**. They connect with the alveoli.

The alveoli have very thin walls. The oxygen in the sacs can pass through. It moves into the capillaries. Inside is a steady stream of blood.

DID YOU KNOW?

It takes energy to move fast. You need more oxygen. That's why you breathe faster when you run. Sit still, and you breathe slowly. You need less energy.

CHAPTER 3

BREATHE OUT

Blood picks up oxygen in the alveoli. But it also drops off **carbon dioxide**. This gas is made when we use oxygen. The gas passes into the alveoli. One gas is exchanged for another.

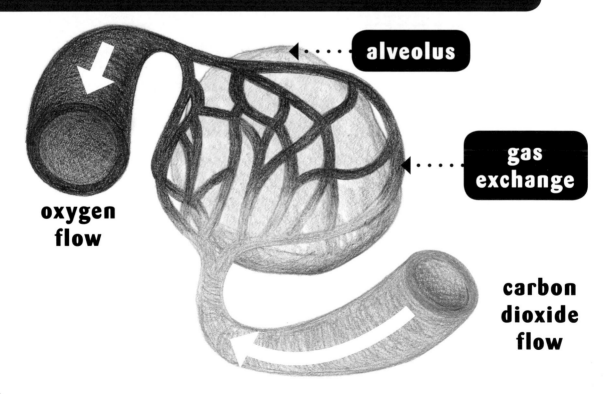

alveolus

gas exchange

oxygen flow

carbon dioxide flow

Now the air in your lungs is out of oxygen. And it's filled with waste. You **exhale** to make space for fresh, clean air.

exhale

THE LUNGS AND THE DIAPHRAGM

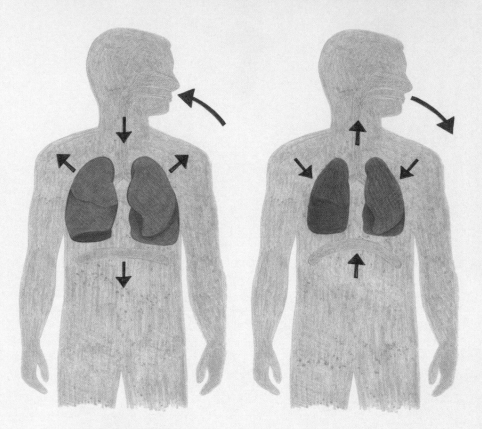

INHALE   EXHALE

When you exhale, your diaphragm relaxes. The muscle pushes up. Now the lungs have less space. Air rushes out of your body.

The respiratory system works with the **circulatory system** to get oxygen through your body. Your heart pumps blood through your veins to send oxygen to every cell in your body.

You breathe in.
You breathe out.
Your body gets the oxygen it needs.

DID YOU KNOW?

Exiting air has another job. It creates your voice! You need air and lungs to speak, sing, shout, and laugh. On its way out, air passes through your **vocal cords**. They **vibrate** to make a sound.

ACTIVITIES & TOOLS

TRY THIS!

MAKE A LUNG

Use a bottle and balloons to make a lung.

What You Need:
- an empty plastic water bottle
- two balloons
- scissors
- a thumbtack

① **Cut off the round end of one balloon.**

② **Stick the thumbtack in the bottom of the water bottle. This makes a hole. Pull the thumbtack out. Be careful!**

③ **Put the cut balloon's round end over the bottom of the bottle. It covers up the hole.**

④ **Blow in the other balloon. Let the air out. This stretches the balloon.**

⑤ **Put the balloon in the top of the bottle. Fold the top of the balloon over the bottle's rim. The balloon now hangs inside the bottle. This is the lung.**

⑥ **Pull on the bottom balloon. This is the diaphragm. What happens to the top balloon?**

GLOSSARY

alveoli: Tiny air sacs in the lungs.

bronchi: Two main tubes that branch off the windpipe.

bronchioles: Smaller tubes that branch off the bronchi.

capillaries: Small tubes that carry blood in the body.

carbon dioxide: A gas that is a waste product of the body.

circulatory system: The system of blood, vessels, and heart that moves blood throughout the body.

diaphragm: A muscle wall between the chest and the abdomen.

exhale: To breathe out.

inhale: To breathe in.

lobes: Rounded parts of something.

lungs: Baglike organs inside your chest that you use to breathe; the lungs supply the blood with oxygen and rid it of carbon dioxide.

mucus: A slimy fluid that coats and protects the inside of your mouth, nose, throat, and other breathing passages.

organs: Parts of the body that do certain jobs.

oxygen: A gas found in the air, which people need to live.

respiratory system: The body system that controls breathing.

vibrate: To move back and forth rapidly, producing a quivering effect or sound.

vocal cords: Tissue in the throat that vibrates to make a person's voice.

INDEX

air 5, 8, 10, 11, 12, 15, 17, 19, 20

alveoli 15, 16

blood 15, 16, 20

breathing 4, 5, 7, 8, 12, 15, 20

bronchi 12

bronchioles 12

capillaries 15

carbon dioxide 16

cells 20

chest 7

circulatory system 20

diaphragm 8, 19

energy 5, 15

exhaling 17, 19

inhaling 8, 10

lobes 8

lungs 7, 8, 12, 15, 17, 19, 20

mucus 11

muscle 8, 19

nose 10

organs 7

oxygen 5, 15, 16, 17, 20

ribs 7

veins 15, 20

vocal cords 20

windpipe 12

TO LEARN MORE

Learning more is as easy as 1, 2, 3.

1) Go to www.factsurfer.com

2) Enter "respiratorysystem" into the search box.

3) Click the "Surf" button to see a list of websites.

With factsurfer, finding more information is just a click away.